# Special Times With God

After reading this book, please give it to someone you love.

# Special Times With God

by
David and Naomi Shibley

Sixth printing

Published in Nashville, Tennessee, by Thomas Nelson, Inc. and distrib-
uted in Canada by Lawson Falle, Ltd., Cambridge, Ontario.

Printed in the United States of America.

Illustrated by May Abers

**Library of Congress Cataloging in Publication Data**

Shibley, David.
  Special times with God.

  Summary: Readings on various subjects with
Bible verses, questions for discussion, and pray-
ers, for use in family devotions.
    1. Family—Prayer books and devotions—English.
[1. Prayer books and devotions]  I. Shibley, Naomi,
II. Title.
BV255.S47       249        81-14116
ISBN 0-8407-5780-8      AACR2

Re-Published 1995

# Contents

## III. Why Jesus Came to Earth

# Special Times With God

# Foreword

Christian parents today are faced with one of the greatest challenges and responsibilities ever undertaken: the godly upbringing of their children. In a culture where Christian values and parental authority are being attacked and undermined on every front, parents cannot take their task too seriously or begin spiritual training too early. Be assured that the principalities and powers of spiritual darkness against which Christian parents must battle are determined to destroy our children from the time they are born.

This book is for parents who have understood and accepted their duty—indeed their privilege—of teaching their children about God and His ways and of leading them into a personal relationship with the Lord Jesus Christ. It is designed for young families who want to begin a tradition of family devotions that are meaningful and fundamental to Christian growth and character. The fifty-eight sessions, which can be covered in a year's time (with extras for special occasions and holidays), lay a solid foundation for a child's future spiritual understanding.

I heartily commend this book to you, and I personally thank David and Naomi Shibley for this valuable contribution to the preservation of Christian family life.

# A Word to Parents

This book grew out of our own need.

We needed help in family devotions. There were several excellent devotional materials available. But we were searching for one book that combined Scripture memory, a brief story, a simple catechism, an aid to family discussion, and an aid to prayer, all reinforcing the basic truth of the gospel. This book is the result.

We studied to find a system for family devotions that is both workable and flexible. In the crucible of our own frustrations, failures, and victories, we arrived at some principles that we're convinced are valid.

1. *Brevity is the key.* When it comes to communicating the faith to young children, multiple short dosages are often best. We had to admit that our own attention span is short. How much more our children's! So we have worked to keep each session no longer than five minutes. We know now that the strength of family devotions lies not in length but in consistency.

2. *Repetition is vital to learning.* The book is divided into seven sections, each section having several sessions. Each session is

designed to be read and reinforced for a week. One major truth is presented each week.

The repetition of a specific truth at spaced intervals yields exciting results. God commanded the parents of Israel to reinforce His truth to their children at four natural points during the day. " 'And these words which I command you today shall be in your heart; you shall teach them diligently to your children, and shall talk of them when you sit in your house, when you walk by the way, when you lie down, and when you rise up' " (Deut. 6:6,7). We try to reinforce the week's memory verse at four times each day.

3. *Children should be taught essential truths of Scripture.* Believing as we do that all spiritual growth is predicated on one's understanding of the character of God, the first section is devoted to that theme.

Obviously the character of God is a vast subject. Parents should feel free to interject their own insights and experiences throughout this section and the entire book. Perhaps no one can be more successful in relating concepts to children than their own parents.

For example, in the session "God Made You" parents may wish to share with the child how they prepared for him even before birth. Share with your child how you prayed for him and how God lovingly answered your prayers. In short, these sessions are not meant to be purely didactic. They are meant to be an impartation of your faith to your child.

We are strong proponents of child evangelism, since both of us were converted at early ages. In our opinion it is never too early to share the gospel with children. America's children suffer not from overexposure to Jesus but from underexposure. So this book is unapologetically evangelistic in tone. Jesus said,

" 'Let the little children come to Me, and do not forbid them; for of such is the kingdom of God' " (Mark 10:14).

In a society that has cut itself loose from its Judeo-Christian moorings and is consequently drowning in the muck of subjectivism, the Ten Commandments will give our children the stability and direction they need and deserve. We also see the Beatitudes as forming a basis for a genuinely Christian system of ethics and behavior.

Right living stems from right thinking. The content of these devotions therefore is strong in Christian doctrine. The Apostles' Creed, a very early baptismal confession, is one of the most universal of all the church's statements. It is a marvelous summary of Christian belief and a deposit of truth to be planted in the child's fertile mind and heart.

4. *Scripture memory is crucial.* King David said, "Your word I have hidden in my heart,/That I might not sin against you" (Ps. 119:11).

While we are grateful for the influx of translations of the Bible, we experienced frustration in deciding which one to use for memorization. Surely, we thought, thousands of other parents had the same problem. Of course, we had been raised with the King James Version and its beauty is still unexcelled. But the wording is sometimes antiquated.

We found an answer to this dilemma in the New King James Bible. It updates obsolete phrases while keeping the sublimity of the Authorized Version intact. For Bible memory it is the answer for our children, so wherever a biblical passage is quoted we have used The New King James Bible.

5. *Life must be imparted!* Books can't do that. They impart information, but that's not enough. Only Jesus Christ can give spiritual life. Our children will see Him, or fail to see Him, as

they scrutinize our lives. We must remain ever mindful that the goal of all our instruction is to see our children experience a vibrant, living relationship with Jesus Christ as their Savior and Lord.

We're still learning how to have more effective family devotions. But we have definitely made a sound beginning. When we began using the contents of this book in our own family time, the results were so encouraging that we had to share them. We've known firsthand the mixture of duty and despair that so many Christian parents feel regarding family devotions. Now we have something to contribute.

Have we been successful? We may not know that answer for many years. But if the early evidence is any indication, never has such a small investment yielded such valuable dividends.

David and Naomi Shibley
*Rockwall, Texas*

# I.

# What God Is Like

# God Made
# the World

**Let's Remember:**
"In the beginning God created the heaven and the earth" (Genesis 1:1).

**Let's Listen:**
Look up! God made the sun, moon, stars, and sky. Look around! God made the trees, plants, and animals. He made pretty flowers. He made food in our gardens. He made the oceans and rivers and fish of the sea. God made people too. He *created* the world. That means He made everything out of nothing.

Everything God made is for His glory. That means that everything everywhere was made to please God.

**Let's Answer:**
Question: Who made everything?

**Answer:** God made everything.

**Let's Talk About It:**
Name some things God made.

**Let's Pray Together:**
Thank You, God, for making everything beautiful. Help me take good care of Your world. Amen.*

---

*These are guides to prayer. Parents should encourage their children in spontaneous expressions of prayer and praise to God.

# God Made You

## Let's Remember:

"I will praise You, for I am fearfully and wonderfully made" (Psalm 139:14).

## Let's Listen:

After God made the world He made a man named Adam and a woman named Eve. All the people of the world came from them.

There is nobody else just like you. God made you special, and He has something important for you to do.

God made people so they could love Him. We call this being made in God's image. This makes people more important than anything else God made.

### Let's Answer:

Question: Who made you?
Answer: God made me.

Question: Why are people so important?
Answer: Because people are made in God's image.

### Let's Talk About It:

You can see your image in a mirror. Who is reflected in the mirror? What do you think it means to be made in God's image?

### Let's Pray Together:

Thank You, God, for making me. Thank You for my body. Thank You for my mind. Thank You that I can know You. I'm glad You have given me something important to do with my life. Help me to live my life for You. Amen.

# God

**Let's Remember:**

" 'Go therefore and make disciples of all the nations, baptizing them in the name of the Father and of the Son and of the Holy Spirit' " (Matthew 28:19).

**Let's Listen:**

There is one God who exists forever. God the Father loves all the people of the world very much. So He sent His Son, Jesus, from heaven to earth to be born as a baby. He died to save us from our sins. The Holy Spirit guides the church and lives inside all true Christians.

God is a trinity. Trinity means "three in one." God the Father, God the Son, and God the Holy Spirit are present with you every day.*

24

### Let's Answer:

Question: What does "trinity" mean?

Answer: Trinity means "three in one."

Question: What three Persons make up the one true God?

Answer: God the Father, God the Son, and God the Holy Spirit.

### Let's Talk About It:

What are some things Jesus did to show us what His Father is like? How can the Holy Spirit guide you?

### Let's Pray Together:

Dear God, You are the one true God. I love You, Father. I love You, Jesus. I love You, Holy Spirit. Amen.

---

*Parents may want to use the analogy of water, ice, and steam to help older children understand the concept of three in one. This can be done by putting ice cubes beside a cup of steaming hot water and explaining that water exists in three ways: solid, liquid, and gas. Likewise God is three persons: the Father, Son and Holy Spirit.

# God Is Love

*Let's Remember:*
"... God is love" (1 John 4:8).

*Let's Listen:*
God the Father loves everyone in the world. He loves you. You are very special to Him. The Father loves you so much that He sent His Son, Jesus, from heaven. God gave His Son to die for you. That's how you can know He loves you. The Bible says, "But God demonstrates His own love toward us, in that while we were still sinners, Christ died for us" (Romans 5:8).

How do you feel toward a person who makes fun of you or hits you? It's hard to love someone like that, isn't it? But God loves us even when we don't love and obey Him. It is a sin not to love and obey God, and

God must punish sin. That's why He sent Jesus to take the punishment for us, because all of us have sinned. You see, God loves us so much, He was willing to be punished in our place. That would be like your asking to be spanked in place of your brother or sister who did something wrong. See how much God loves you?

### Let's Answer:
Question:   How do you know God the Father loves you?

Answer:   He sent Jesus to die for me.

### Let's Talk About It:
Some people think God doesn't love them. How do we know He does love them?

### Let's Pray Together:
Thank You, God, for loving me. Thank You for sending Jesus to die for me. This shows me how much You love me. Amen.

# God Is Holy

"But as He who has called you is holy, you also be holy in all your conduct . . ." (1 Peter 1:15).

**Let's Listen:**
God is holy. He is like no one else. That's because He thinks and does only what is right. God wants us to be holy too. That means He wants us to belong to Him and to love and obey Him. Instead of thinking bad thoughts, He wants us to think good thoughts. Instead of doing wrong things, He wants us to do what is right and good. God can help us do the right things. God is happy when we ask Him to make us holy. And we are happy too.

***Let's Answer:***

Question:   What does it mean to be holy?

Answer:    To be holy means to belong to God and to love and obey Him.

***Let's Talk About It:***

God has never done anything wrong. This is because He is holy. He wants to make us holy too. When are some times you need God to help you be holy? For example, what should you do if someone says mean things about you?

***Let's Pray Together:***

Thank You, God, for being holy. I'm glad that You think and do only what is right. Help me to live like that too. Amen.

# God Is
# Our Father

## Let's Remember:

"But as many as received [Jesus], to them He gave the right to become children of God . . ." (John 1:12).

## Let's Listen:

Not everyone has God for their Father. Jesus told the Pharisees, "You are of your father, the devil. . ." (John 8:44). But when someone invites Jesus into his life, God becomes his Father in heaven. Most of us have fathers living here with us on earth. How wonderful that we can have God as our Father too! He loves us even more than our fathers on earth love us. He always is able to give us what we need. He will take care of us perfectly.

*Let's Answer:*
   Question:   When does God become your Father?
   Answer:      When I receive Jesus into my life.

*Let's Talk About It:*
What are some ways God is a good Father to us?

*Let's Pray Together:*
Jesus taught us to pray in this way.

> Our Father in heaven,
> Hallowed be Your name.
> Your kingdom come.
> Your will be done
> On earth as it is in heaven.
> Give us this day our daily bread.
> And forgive us our debts,
> As we forgive our debtors.
> And do not lead us into temptation,
> But deliver us from the evil one.
> For Yours is the kingdom
>    and the power
>    and the glory forever. Amen.
>                    (Matthew 6:9–13)

# God's Son Is Jesus

**Let's Remember:**

"Simon Peter answered and said, 'You are the Christ, the Son of the living God' " (Matthew 16:16).

**Let's Listen:**

Jesus is God and He is also human. This is difficult to understand, and even adults can't explain it. They can only say that the Bible teaches it. The Bible calls this a mystery.

God arranged to have Jesus be born just like any other baby. He grew up like us. Since Jesus is a Man, He was sometimes tired and hungry. But since Jesus is God, He never did one thing that was sinful or wrong. Jesus is God's special-born Son who lived forever with His Father in heaven before coming to earth. The Bible calls Him God's "only begotten Son." Jesus is today God and Man all at once.

**Let's Answer:**
    Question:   Who is God's special-born Son?
    Answer:     Jesus is God's special-born Son.

**Let's Talk About It:**
    Name some ways that Jesus is special and like no one else.

**Let's Pray Together:**
    Thank You, Jesus, for showing me what Your Father is like. I know God the Father loves me because You love me and You are God and Man both at once. I believe that You were special-born from heaven, that You were born on earth and are the Son of the living God. Amen.

# God's Spirit Is in Our World

**Let's Remember:**

" 'When . . . the Spirit of truth has come, He will guide you into all truth. . .' " (John 16:13).

**Let's Listen:**

We call God's Spirit the Holy Spirit. The Holy Spirit lets people know they need Jesus in their life. After a person becomes a Christian the Holy Spirit comes and lives inside and makes him able to be the kind of person that makes God the Father happy. He gives special gifts to Christians. He also helps them live like Jesus.

**Let's Answer:**

Question: Who makes people know they need Jesus in their life?

| | |
|---|---|
| Answer: | The Holy Spirit. |
| Question: | Who makes Christians able to live a life that pleases God? |
| Answer: | The Holy Spirit. |

**Let's Talk About It:**

What do you need the Holy Spirit to help you do?

**Let's Pray Together:**

Holy Spirit, You are God; just as Jesus is God and the Father is God. Help me to know when You speak to me and help me to obey You. Amen.

# II.

## God Gave Rules
## for a Good Life

# You Shall Have No Other Gods Before Me

**Let's Remember:**

" 'You shall have no other gods before Me' " (Exodus 20:3).

**Let's Listen:**

God gave rules to Moses for the people of Israel to obey. We call these rules the Ten Commandments. When we obey God's commands, we make God happy.

The first rule commands us to worship and serve only God. No person or thing should take the first place in our lives that only God deserves. We must never let anyone or anything be more important to us than God.

## Let's Answer:

Question: Who should be most important in your life?

Answer: God should be most important in my life.

## Let's Talk About It:

What are some things that could become more important to us than God, if we let them?

## Let's Pray Together:

Dear God, I will worship and serve You alone. May nothing ever be more important to me than You. Amen.

# You Shall Not Make Any Graven Image

**Let's Remember:**
" 'You shall not make for yourself any graven image...' " (Exodus 20:4).

**Let's Listen:**
Some people don't worship the true and living God. They worship gods they make themselves: statues of wood, stone, and metal. These statues aren't the real God. They cannot hear or answer when people pray to them. They are false gods. The Bible calls them "graven images" or "idols."

But an idol can be *anything* that becomes more important to us than God. We must not have any idols in our lives.

*Let's Answer:*

    Question:   What is an idol?

    Answer:     An idol is anything that is more important to me than God.

*Let's Talk About It:*

What are some things that could become idols in your life?

*Let's Pray Together:*

Dear God, You are the true and living God. May I never have any idol in my life. I will love and serve You with my whole heart. Amen.

# You Shall Not Take the Name of the Lord Your God in Vain

**Let's Remember:**

" 'You shall not take the name of the LORD your God in vain. . .' " (Exodus 20:7).

**Let's Listen:**

When people use God's name without proper respect, they are taking His name in vain. People sometimes curse using the name of God the Father or Jesus His Son. God clearly commands us not to do this. God promises that those who take His name in vain will one day answer to Him for it.

When we speak God's name we must always remember that He is the almighty God, the Ruler of heaven and earth. His name is always to be spoken with respect.

***Let's Answer:***

  Question: What does it mean to take God's name in vain?

  Answer: When people speak God's name without proper respect, they are taking His name in vain.

***Let's Talk About It:***

How can we make sure we will never take God's name in vain?

***Let's Pray Together:***

Help me, Lord, to be very careful what I say. May I always respect and honor You and Your name in all that I say and do. Amen.

# Remember the Sabbath Day to Keep It Holy

**Let's Remember:**

" 'Remember the sabbath day, to keep it holy' " (Exodus 20:8).

**Let's Listen:**

God rested on the seventh day after He had created the heavens, earth, and man. He has told us, too, to take one day of rest each week.

Most Christians worship together on Sundays to celebrate that Jesus rose from the dead on the first day of the week. This is our special day for the Lord, and it should be a day set aside for God. On that day we should worship God, remember all the wonderful things He has done, and rest with our family.

*Let's Answer:*

Question: How can you keep Sunday holy?

Answer: By worshiping God, remembering all the wonderful things He has done, and resting with my family.

*Let's Talk About It:*

What should our family do to keep the sabbath day holy?

*Let's Pray Together:*

Dear God, help me to remember to make Sunday a special day just for You. Amen.

# Honor Your Father and Your Mother

**Let's Remember:**

" 'Honor your father and your mother, that your days may be long upon the land. . .' " (Exodus 20:12).

**Let's Listen:**

God gave us parents because He loves us. God uses parents to bring us into His world and to protect us and to help us love and obey God.

We honor our parents by obeying them. We should always be respectful of them and do what they say. We should try to please our parents by doing what we know is right. This pleases God, too. He rewards those who honor their parents with long life.

**Let's Answer:**

Question:   How do you honor your parents?

**Answer:** I honor my parents by obeying them and respecting them.

### *Let's Talk About It:*
What are some ways that you could show that you honor your parents?

### *Let's Pray Together:*
Thank You, God, for my parents. Help me to always respect them and obey them. Amen.

# You Shall Not Murder

***Let's Remember:***

" 'You shall not murder' " (Exodus 20:13).

***Let's Listen:***

Every person is very special to God. Even before we were born, God knew about us, cared about us, and loved us. Since God has given us life, we should never plan to take life away, ours or anyone else's.

We are to respect our own lives and the lives of others. God gave every person the great gift of life. We are to protect this wonderful gift.

***Let's Answer:***

Question:   Who gave you life?
Answer:     God gave me life.

Question:   How should you treat this gift of life?
Answer:     I should thank God for life. I should respect life. I should protect life.

### Let's Talk About It:

What are some ways you can show respect for your own life and for the lives of others?

### Let's Pray Together:

Thank You, God, for my life and for the lives of others. May I always respect and protect the lives of all people. Amen.

# You Shall Not Commit Adultery

**Let's Remember:**

" 'You shall not commit adultery' " (Exodus 20:14).

**Let's Listen:**

God loves families very much. He gave rules to keep families happy. Adultery is when a husband or wife lives with someone other than the person he or she married. This makes many people sad. God says, "Don't!"

How happy we are when we obey God's rules! God is happy with us, and we are happy with ourselves.

**Let's Answer:**

Question:   Why should people never commit adultery?

Answer: Because God commands us not to commit adultery. He knows it makes many people sad.

## Let's Talk About It:

When you grow up, God may want you to get married. If He does, He will want you to love and live with the person you marry for the rest of your life. That means loving that person even when he or she is mean or selfish. Who loves us that way? How can we learn to love others no matter what they do or say to us?

## Let's Pray Together:

Dear God, I pray that You will keep me pure in my thoughts and in my body. If one day You want me to marry, give me a happy Christian home where we all can love and serve You. Amen.

# You Shall Not Steal

**Let's Remember:**

" 'You shall not steal' " (Exodus 20:15).

**Let's Listen:**

Stealing is taking something that belongs to someone else. When someone takes something that isn't his, God sees it and He is not pleased.

Stealing is against God's law. It is sin. It is also against the laws of our country. So never take things that don't belong to you.

**Let's Answer:**

Question: What is stealing?
Answer: Stealing is taking something that belongs to someone else.

**Let's Talk About It:**

Why is it wrong to steal? What can happen to peo ple who steal?

**Let's Pray Together:**

Dear God, help me always to be careful with what belongs to others. May I never take anything that isn't mine. Amen.

# You Shall Not Bear False Witness

**Let's Remember:**
" 'You shall not bear false witness. . .' " (Exodus 20:16).

**Let's Listen:**
"Bearing false witness" means saying something that isn't true. It is lying. God commands us not to lie. Telling the truth is very important to God.

Sometimes people lie to get others in trouble. Sometimes people lie because they are afraid to tell the truth. For whatever reason, it is never right to lie. God always wants us to tell the truth.

**Let's Answer:**
Question: What does it mean to bear false witness?

**Answer:** To bear false witness means to say something that isn't true.

### Let's Talk About It:

Sometimes it seems that it would be easier to lie than to tell the truth. When are some of those times? Remember that even in those times we should tell the truth. It's always *better* to tell the truth. Why is that true?

### Let's Pray Together:

Dear God, help me to always tell the truth, even when I want to lie. Amen.

# You Shall Not Covet

**Let's Remember:**
" 'You shall not covet. . .' " (Exodus 20:17).

**Let's Listen:**
"Boy, I wish I could have *his* toys!"

Have you ever heard anyone say that? That's an example of what the Bible calls coveting. Coveting is wanting something that belongs to someone else. Coveting often leads to stealing. Instead of coveting, we should thank God for what we already have. We should be glad other people have what they have.

**Let's Answer:**

| | |
|---|---|
| Question: | What is coveting? |
| Answer: | Coveting is wanting something that belongs to someone else. |

**Let's Talk About It:**

Name some things we often covet.

**Let's Pray Together:**

Thank You, God, for everything You have given me. Help me not to wish for anything that belongs to someone else. Amen.

# III.

# Why Jesus Came to Earth

# Sin and God's Love

***Let's Remember:***
"For all have sinned and fall short of the glory of God" (Romans 3:23).

***Let's Listen:***
Adam and Eve disobeyed God in the Garden of Eden. People have been disobeying God ever since then. When we do not obey God, we are sinning. Sometimes we sin by what we think. Sometimes we sin by what we do.

God hates sin. He must punish our sin. Because of sin people die. Because of sin people are separated from God forever.

But God did not want us to be separated from Him. So He sent His own Son, Jesus, to take the punishment that we deserved. Our sins are forgiven when

60

we turn from them and ask Jesus into our lives. Just think how much God loves us!

*Let's Answer:*
    Question:    What is sin?
    Answer:    Sin is not obeying God.

    Question:    Has everybody sinned?
    Answer:    Yes. Romans 3:23 says, "*All* have sinned. . . ."

*Let's Talk About It:*
What are some ways that people don't obey God?

*Let's Pray Together:*
    Thank You, God, for loving me even though I have sinned. Thank You for sending Jesus to take the punishment for my sins. Amen.

# Baby Jesus

*Let's Remember:*

" 'For God so loved the world that He gave His only begotten Son, that whoever believes in Him should not perish but have everlasting life' " (John 3:16).

*Let's Listen:*

God looked down on the earth and saw all the people disobeying Him. But He still loved them! God the Father loves all people. He doesn't want anyone to die and be punished forever.

So God sent Jesus, His wonderful eternal Son, to be punished for our sins. He came to earth as a little baby. He was born in a manger where animals lived. God was His Father, and Mary was Jesus' mother. Jesus was God's special-born Son, who was born to Mary on earth.

God chose Joseph, Mary's husband, to help care for Jesus when He was a child. An angel told Joseph, "'. . . You shall call His name JESUS, for He will save His people from their sins'" (Matthew 1:21).

Jesus was born in the little town of Bethlehem. That was the world's most wonderful night!

**Let's Answer:**
Question:   Why did God send Jesus to earth?
Answer:     Because He loved us enough to send His Son to be punished in our place.

**Let's Talk About It:**
What made Jesus such a special baby?

**Let's Pray Together:**
Thank You, Jesus, for coming all the way from heaven. Thank You for being born as a little baby. I'm glad you know what it's like to be my age too. Amen.

# Jesus Grew Too!

*Let's Remember:*
"And Jesus increased in wisdom and stature, and in favor with God and men" (Luke 2:52).

*Let's Listen:*
When Jesus was a child He grew just as you are growing. He became wiser as He grew older. His body got bigger and stronger. Jesus loved His Father in heaven and other people. And God was very pleased with Jesus too.

Jesus enjoyed being with other children. He also liked to go with Mary and Joseph to the temple to worship God, His Father.

Because Jesus grew just as you are, He knows what it is like to be your age. You can always talk to Jesus, because He will understand.

***Let's Answer:***

    Question:   How did Jesus grow as a child?

    Answer:     Jesus grew in His mind and in His body. He also grew in favor with God and people.

***Let's Talk About It:***

    Does Jesus understand what it's like to be your age? Why?

***Let's Pray Together:***

    Thank You, Jesus, that You know what it's like to be my age. Help me to grow as You did. Amen.

# Jesus Did Wonderful Things

**Let's Remember:**

"And Jesus went about all Galilee, teaching in their synagogues, preaching the gospel of the kingdom, and healing all kinds of sickness and all kinds of disease among the people" (Matthew 4:23).

**Let's Listen:**

Jesus did many wonderful things. The people loved to listen to Him. He told them the good news that what they had waited to see for so long was now here. God's Son, their Savior, had come.

How exciting it was when Jesus came to town! Jesus did many miracles. A miracle is something only God can do. He made blind people to see and crippled people to walk. Many people had been made sad and afraid by the Devil. Jesus took their fear away and made them happy again. When Jesus touched people they were never the same again.

### Let's Answer:
Question: Jesus did many miracles. What is a miracle?

Answer: A miracle is something only God can do.

### Let's Talk About It:
Name some wonderful things that Jesus did while He was here on earth. Name some wonderful things that Jesus is still doing.

### Let's Pray Together:
Thank You, Jesus, for caring about people. I'm glad that You care when we are hurt or sad or afraid. I'm glad that You can change us and make us well, happy, and not afraid. Amen.

# Jesus Died for You

**Let's Remember:**
". . . Christ died for our sins according to the Scriptures, and . . . He was buried, and . . . He rose again the third day according to the Scriptures" (1 Corinthians 15:3,4).

**Let's Listen:**
Jesus never did anything wrong. But when He grew up, some people didn't like what He was saying and doing. So, they made plans to kill Him. When they arrested Jesus and brought Him to Pilate, the Roman ruler, he said he did not believe Jesus had done anything wrong. But the people yelled, "Crucify Him!" So Pilate allowed Jesus to be nailed to the cross.

But first the soldiers whipped Jesus' back. A crown of large thorns was pressed onto His head. Then Jesus carried His own cross as far as He could toward

Mount Calvary. There the soldiers put nails through His hands and feet. The people spit on Him and laughed at Him. But even then He loved them! He said, " 'Father, forgive them, for they do not know what they do' " (Luke 23:34).

Just before He died, Jesus said, " 'It is finished' " (John 19:30). He took the full punishment for all our sins on the cross. He died for all people everywhere. But He also died just for you.

### Let's Answer:

Question:  What did Jesus mean when He said, "It is finished"?

Answer:  Jesus meant that He had taken the full punishment for all our sins.

### Let's Talk About It:

It looked like the Devil had won when Jesus died on the cross. But he didn't win. Jesus really won, and so did we. Why is that true?

### Let's Pray Together:

Dear Jesus, You love me much more than I could ever understand. Thank You for dying for me. Thank You for taking the punishment for my sins. Amen.

# Jesus Is Alive!

**Let's Remember:**
" 'I am He who lives, and was dead, and behold, I am alive forevermore. Amen. . .' " (Revelation 1:18).

**Let's Listen:**
Three days after Jesus died, some women went to His tomb. They were amazed to see an angel there who said, " 'He is not here! For He is risen as He said' " (Matthew 28:6). The women ran to tell Jesus' followers, the disciples, this wonderful news. The disciples didn't believe them. But Peter and John ran to Jesus' tomb to see for themselves. It was true! He had risen, just as He had promised.

Jesus is still alive today. All power has been given to Him. He is the mighty ruler of heaven and earth. Death and hell could not hold Him. He broke free!

*Let's Answer:*

Question:   Is Jesus alive today?

Answer:   Yes! Jesus is alive today (recite Revelation 1:18).

*Let's Talk About It:*

Because Jesus rose from the dead, what will happen to His followers when they die?

*Let's Pray Together:*

Dear Jesus, I'm glad I don't worship someone who is dead and cannot hear me. Many people in the world pray to false gods like that. I'm thankful that You are alive! You really hear me when I talk to You. Because You live forever, I can live forever, too. Amen.

# Jesus Is Coming Back

***Let's Remember:***

" 'And if I go and prepare a place for you, I will come again and receive you to Myself; that where I am, there you may be also' " (John 14:3).

***Let's Listen:***

Jesus promised that one day He would come back to earth again. When He returns, He won't come as a little baby. This time He will come as the mighty King of Kings and Lord of Lords. Wicked men will no longer be in control. There will be peace throughout all the world. Children won't be afraid anymore. Jesus will rule the earth with His great love.

When that happens, loud voices in heaven will say, " 'The kingdoms of this world have become the kingdoms of our Lord and of His Christ, and He shall reign forever and ever!' " (Revelation 11:15). What a wonderful time that will be!

**Let's Answer:**
   Question:   Who will one day rule over the earth?
   Answer:      Jesus will one day rule over the earth.

**Let's Talk About It:**
   What do you think it will be like when Jesus rules over the earth?

**Let's Pray Together:**
   Thank You, Jesus, that one day You will rule over the whole earth. I'm glad I know that one day You will make everything right. Amen.

# Jesus Is the Only Way to God

**Let's Remember:**

"Jesus said to him, 'I am the way, the truth, and the life. No one comes to the Father except through Me' " (John 14:6).

**Let's Listen:**

There are many religions in the world. They were started by men, not by God. Only Jesus is both God and Man at once. Only Jesus died to take the punishment for our sins. Only Jesus rose from the dead. Only Jesus will one day return for His people, the church.

Many sincere people try to reach God by some way other than Jesus. But Jesus said He is the only way to God. We cannot get to heaven unless we come God's way. The way to God is through His Son Jesus Christ.

Jesus said, " 'I am the door. If anyone enters by Me, he will be saved . . .' " (John 10:9).

Because Jesus is the only way to heaven, the church sends missionaries all over the world to tell people that fact. They tell people the good news that God sent His Son to die for them and to bring them to His kingdom. If they believe in Him, they will not die but will live forever (read or recite John 3:16).

### Let's Answer:

Question: Who is the only way to God and heaven?

Answer: Jesus is the only way to God and heaven.

### Let's Talk About It:

Since Jesus is the only way to God and heaven, how should we feel about those who haven't heard the good news about Jesus? (read Romans 1:14–16).

### Let's Pray Together:

Thank You, Jesus, for opening the way to God for everyone who trusts You. You are the only way to God and to heaven. Amen.

# Jesus Is
# Lord and Savior*

**Let's Remember:**

"That if you confess with your mouth the Lord Jesus and believe in your heart that God has raised Him from the dead, you will be saved . . . For 'whoever calls upon the name of the Lord will be saved'" (Romans 10:9,13).

**Let's Listen:**

It's important to know *about* Jesus, but it's even more important for you to *know* Him. You can know Jesus by turning from your sins and inviting Him to

---

*Parents will need to be sensitive to their child's readiness and to the Holy Spirit's leading as they begin this devotional session. The "Let's Talk About It" and "Let's Pray Together" sections may need to be altered if the child has already accepted Christ or if he or she appears not to understand the significance of this act. Parents must avoid having the child pray the prayer simply to please them.

rule your life. The Bible calls this being saved or born again.

You know that Jesus is God's special-born Son. You know that He never sinned but that He took the punishment for your sins when He died on the cross. You know that God raised Him from the dead and that one day He will come back. You know that Jesus is the only way to God and heaven.

Jesus will come into your life if you will ask Him. When you ask Him into your life, you become God's child and part of God's family. The Bible says, "But as many as received Him, to them He gave the right to become children of God, even to those who believe in His name" (John 1:12).

### Let's Answer:

Question:  How can you know Jesus?

Answer:  I can know Jesus by turning from my sins and inviting Him into my life.

### Let's Talk About It:

Jesus is waiting for you to invite Him into your life. The Bible says, ". . . Behold, now is the accepted time; behold, now is the day of salvation" (2 Corinthians

6:2). Will you turn from your sins and ask Jesus to rule your life right now?

*Let's Pray Together:*

You can invite Jesus to come into your life right now. You can say something like this:

"Lord Jesus, thank You for dying for me. I'm sorry for my sins. I turn away from them now, and I turn to You. I trust You and You alone to get to heaven. I take You now as my personal Savior. I will follow You as my Lord for the rest of my life. Thank You for hearing my prayer, forgiving my sins, and coming into my life. Amen."

Welcome to God's wonderful family! You have received Jesus and He has received you. Jesus said, " 'All that the Father gives Me will come to Me, and the one who comes to Me I will by no means cast out' " (John 6:37). Now you can know Jesus even better!

# Jesus Is Praying for You

## Let's Remember:

"Therefore He is also able to save to the uttermost those who come to God by Him, seeing He ever lives to make intercession for them" (Hebrews 7:25).

## Let's Listen:

Jesus stayed on the earth for forty days after He rose from the dead. He told His disciples that He had to go back to heaven but that He and His Father would send the Holy Spirit to them in His place. The disciples were to go into all the nations and tell everyone the wonderful news about what Jesus had done for them. Jesus told the disciples that they were to teach people everywhere all that He had taught them. The Holy Spirit would help them with this task.

After Jesus told them these things, He was taken up

into heaven. There He sat down at the right hand of God His Father. From that time until now Jesus has been asking God the Father to bless all those who have believed in Him. Just think, if you're a Christian, Jesus is talking to God about you!

## Let's Answer:
Question:   What is Jesus doing in heaven?
Answer:      Jesus is praying for those who believe in Him.

## Let's Talk About It:
It's so good to know that when a Christian makes a mistake, Jesus asks for forgiveness for him! What are some things that you think Jesus talks to God the Father about?

## Let's Pray Together:
Dear Jesus, I'm glad that You keep on caring about us. You cared for people while You were on the earth. But You still care for us now that You're in heaven. I'm glad that You talk to God about all of those who believe in You. Amen.

# Jesus,
## the Good Shepherd

**Let's Remember:**

"I will both lie down in peace, and sleep; for You alone, O LORD, make me dwell in safety" (Psalm 4:8).

**Let's Listen:**

Sometimes people with sin in their lives do mean things to hurt other people. The Lord Jesus is able to protect you from every evil. That means He is able to keep you safe. You don't have to be afraid of anything because He is strong enough to protect you.

The shepherd boy David knew the Lord would protect him. He wrote:

> The Lord is my shepherd;
>  I shall not want.
> He makes me to lie down
>  in green pastures;

He leads me beside
   the still waters.
He restores my soul;
He leads me in the paths
   of righteousness
For His name's sake.

Yea, though I walk
   through the valley
     of the shadow of death,
I will fear no evil;
For You are with me;
Your rod and Your staff,
   they comfort me.
You prepare a table before me
   in the presence of my enemies;
You anoint my head with oil;
My cup runs over.

Surely goodness and mercy
   shall follow me
     all the days of my life;
And I will dwell
   in the house of the LORD
Forever (Psalm 23).

***Let's Answer:***

Question:   Why don't you need to be afraid?
Answer:     Because God is able to protect me.

***Let's Talk About It:***

What are some things you've been afraid of? Why don't you need to be afraid of them anymore?

***Let's Pray Together:***

Thank You, Lord Jesus, that You will keep me safe. I'm so glad that You are always with me. Now I don't have to be afraid. Amen.

# IV.

## *God's Spirit Makes Us Like Jesus*

# God's Spirit Brings Love

**Let's Remember:**

"But the fruit of the Spirit is love. . ." (Galatians 5:22).

**Let's Listen:**

When a person invites Jesus into his life, the Holy Spirit begins to change him. God's Spirit begins to work inside the new Christian so he will think and act like Jesus.

When we let Jesus change us, we begin to love people more. Jesus takes hate and envy away. In its place, He gives us His love. Jesus said, " 'By this all will know that you are My disciples, if you have love for one another' " (John 13:35).

**Let's Answer:**

Question:   How will people know if you are a follower of Jesus?

Answer:   People will know I am a follower of Jesus by my love for all people.

**Let's Talk About It:**

Jesus gives His people love for other people. Who are some people you want Jesus to give you love for?

**Let's Pray Together:**

Thank You, Father, for sending the Holy Spirit to make me think and act like Jesus. I want You to change me so that I can love people as You do. Amen.

# God's Spirit Brings Joy

***Let's Remember:***
"But the fruit of the Spirit is love, joy. . ." (Galatians 5:22).

***Let's Listen:***
Christians have problems just like anyone else. But Christians have Jesus as their constant Friend. He goes through the problems with us. The Holy Spirit gives us joy when we're in trouble.

Of course, there are times when we are sad. But even then we can have joy, because we know that when things go wrong for Christians God causes everything to work out in a good way in the end (read Romans 8:28).

**Let's Answer:**

Question: Do Christians have problems?
Answer: Yes.

Question: Why can Christians have joy even when things go wrong?
Answer: Because God will work everything out in a good way in the end.

**Let's Talk About It:**

What are some problems or troubles you have? Even then, how can you have the joy of the Lord?

**Let's Pray Together:**

Thank You, Lord Jesus, that even in times of trouble I can have Your joy in my heart. It brings me joy just to think that I know You. I love You. Amen.

# God's Spirit
# Brings Peace

**Let's Remember:**
   "But the fruit of the Spirit is love, joy, peace. . ."
(Galatians 5:22).

**Let's Listen:**
   Most people want their lives to be peaceful. "Peace" means not fighting or arguing with others, and it means not being afraid of or angry with God. People fight with each other because they are fighting within themselves. People who don't know God don't have peace inside. When we come to God by inviting Jesus into our lives, we have peace with God. As we obey the Lord, the peace of God takes the place of our fears and makes us feel safe.
   Jesus promised His disciples, " 'Peace I leave with you, My peace I give to you; not as the world gives do I

give to you. Let not your heart be troubled, neither let it be afraid' " (John 14:27).

### Let's Answer:
Question: What does "peace" mean?

Answer: It means not fighting or arguing with others and not being afraid of or angry with God.

Question: Why do people fight with each other?

Answer: Because people are fighting within themselves.

Question: How do we make peace with God?

Answer: We make peace with God by inviting Jesus into our lives.

### Let's Talk About It:
What kind of peace does Jesus give us?

### Let's Pray Together:
Thank You, Lord Jesus, for giving me peace inside. Because I know You, I have peace with You. Because I am at peace with You and with myself, I can be at peace with others. Amen.

# God's Spirit Brings Longsuffering

**Let's Remember:**

"But the fruit of the Spirit is love, joy, peace, longsuffering. . ." (Galatians 5:22).

**Let's Listen:**

To be longsuffering means to be patient. To be patient means to trust God and to love others even when things don't go our way. Just think how patient Jesus is with us. When we sin, He forgives us because He loves us. Even when we say we're sorry and then sin again, He keeps forgiving us. Since He lives inside those of us who love Him, we can be patient and understanding, too, when other people say or do things that hurt us.

The Bible says, "Be kind to one another, tenderhearted, forgiving one another, even as God for Christ's sake has forgiven you" (Ephesians 4:32).

### Let's Answer:

Question: What does it mean to be longsuffering?

Answer: To be longsuffering means to be patient.

### Let's Talk About It:

Who are some people with whom you need to be patient?

### Let's Pray Together:

Thank You, Lord Jesus, for the strength to be patient with others. Thank You so much for being patient with me. Amen.

# God's Spirit
# Brings Kindness

**Let's Remember:**

"But the fruit of the Spirit is love, joy, peace, long-suffering, kindness. . ." (Galatians 5:22).

**Let's Listen:**

Jesus was always kind to people who were hurting. He cared how they felt and wanted them to be happy and well. Since we want to be like Jesus, we will care how others feel too. The Holy Spirit will help us to be kind by saying and doing what will make others glad.

**Let's Answer:**

Question: How can you show kindness?
Answer: I can show kindness by saying and doing what will make others glad.

## Let's Talk About It:

Name someone who needs to be shown kindness today. How can you show this person kindness?

## Let's Pray Together:

Thank You, Jesus, for always being so kind to me. And thank You for helping me be kind to others. Amen.

# God's Spirit Brings Goodness

**Let's Remember:**

"But the fruit of the Spirit is love, joy, peace, long-suffering, kindness, goodness. . ." (Galatians 5:22).

**Let's Listen:**

Jesus is the only person who ever lived who was always truly good. But now Jesus' Spirit lives inside of us! So *His* goodness can be lived out through *us!*

To be good means that we think, say, and do what pleases God. God's Spirit works in us to produce goodness. The Bible says that those who trust Jesus as their Savior are "created in Christ Jesus for good works" (Ephesians 2:10).

**Let's Remember:**

Question: What is goodness?

Answer: Goodness is thinking, saying, and doing what pleases God.

### Let's Talk About It:

Who is the only person who ever lived who was always good? Does He now live inside of you? Then His goodness is inside you, isn't it? Let's ask Jesus to let His goodness show through us.

### Let's Pray Together:*

Lord Jesus, I'm so thankful You live inside of me since I've invited You into my life. I want You to live Your life through mine. Thank You for the Holy Spirit who works to make me like You. Amen.

---

*If the child has not yet prayed to receive Christ as Savior, you may want to read again the session entitled "Jesus Is Lord" on page 76. Or you may want to alter the prayer to better fit the child's situation.

# God's Spirit Brings Faithfulness

***Let's Remember:***

"But the fruit of the Spirit is love, joy, peace, long-suffering, kindness, goodness, faithfulness. . ." (Galatians 5:22).

***Let's Listen:***

The Bible speaks many times about the need for Christians to be faithful. When someone is faithful he can be trusted. When a person is faithful he can be depended on. A faithful person can be counted on to do what he says he will do.

We should first be faithful to God. We show Him our faithfulness by how we live every day. If we learn to read the Bible and obey it, if we pray, if we tell others about Jesus, if we go to church whenever we can, we are showing faithfulness to God.

We should also be faithful to those around us. We should always be loyal to our family and friends and never say anything unkind about them. When we tell someone we will do something for them, we should do it! This will show that we can be trusted and that we are faithful.

*Let's Answer:*

Question: How can you know if a person is faithful?

Answer: When a person is faithful he can be trusted to do what he says he will do.

*Let's Talk About It:*

The Bible says that God can be trusted to keep His promises (read 1 Thessalonians 5:24; 1 John 1:9). If we can trust God to keep His promises, shouldn't others be able to trust us as God's children to keep our promises? What are some ways that you can show faithfulness?

*Let's Pray Together:*

Dear God, make me a faithful person by Your Holy Spirit. I want You and other people to know I can be depended on to do those things I promise to do. Amen.

# God's Spirit Brings Gentleness

**Let's Remember:**

"But the fruit of the Spirit is love, joy, peace, long-suffering, kindness, goodness, faithfulness, gentleness . . ." (Galatians 5:22,23).

**Let's Listen:**

People can sometimes be mean and cruel. They can shout bad things that hurt others. They can be unkind and hateful in the way they act. Often people act mean because they have been treated mean. Most of those who try to hurt others have been hurt in some way themselves.

So when people are mean to us, we should not be mean to them. Instead, we should be gentle and try to understand that they probably are hurting inside. We should always remember the Golden Rule that Jesus gave us: " 'Therefore, whatever you want men to do to you, you also do to them . . .' " (Matthew 7:12). That's the best way to live!

### Let's Answer:

Question: What is the Golden Rule?

Answer: " 'Whatever you want men to do to you, you also do to them . . .' " (Matthew 7:12).

### Let's Talk About It:

Can you think of someone who has not been nice to you? How should you act toward that person?

### Let's Pray Together:

Dear God, help me to always remember the Golden Rule and to live by what it says. Make me truly gentle to all people. Amen.

# God's Spirit Brings Self-Control

*Let's Remember:*

"But the fruit of the Spirit is love, joy, peace, long-suffering, kindness, goodness, faithfulness, gentleness, self-control" (Galatians 5:22,23).

*Let's Listen:*

Self-control means that we are able to control how we act. If a person is self-controlled he doesn't pout or throw temper tantrums. He doesn't eat too much food. He isn't controlled by bad habits.

When Jesus is Lord of every part of our lives, we have self-control. The person who is self-controlled is learning to do what is right even when he doesn't feel like it. What he wants doesn't control him. God controls him.

We have been learning about the fruit which the

Holy Spirit makes to grow in our lives. Some people call the different parts of this fruit *Christian virtues.* That just means that the Holy Spirit helps us live more and more like Jesus, as we let Him control our lives.

## Let's Answer:

Question: What is self-control?

Answer: Self-control means that I am able to control how I act.

Question: How can you have self-control?

Answer: I can have self-control by letting Jesus be the Lord of every part of my life.

Question: Who makes Christian virtues grow in you?

Answer: The Holy Spirit makes Christian virtues grow in me.

## Let's Talk About It:

What are some times when you feel unable to control how you act? If you have asked Jesus to come into your life, you can do what is right at those times even when you don't feel like it. Ask Jesus to help you.

*Let's Pray Together:*

Lord Jesus, You know the times when I need self-control. I'm asking You now to be Lord of those times. Thank You that Your Spirit makes self-control grow in those people who love You. Amen.

# V.

## How to Make God Happy

# Faith in God

**Let's Remember:**
"Without faith it is impossible to please [God] . . ."
(Hebrews 11:6).

**Let's Listen:**
We become Christians by faith in Jesus Christ. To have faith means to believe in something we can't see, touch, or hear and to know without a doubt that what we believe is true. Faith is a gift that we can ask God for.

Christians show God that they have faith in Him by believing and doing what He says in His Word, the Bible. This pleases God. God is also pleased when we trust Him to take care of us and to know what is best for us.

You can show that you have faith in God by praying

106

to Him, by telling your friends about Jesus, by obeying your parents, and by doing whatever you know will please your Father in heaven.

### Let's Answer:
Question: What does it mean to have faith in God?

Answer: To have faith in God means to believe in Him even though I can't see Him and to do and believe what He says in the Bible.

### Let's Talk About It:
There is one thing that we *must* have to please God. What is it?

### Let's Pray Together:
Thank You, Lord Jesus, for the gift of faith in You. Please give me faith to believe in You always and to trust You to take care of me in the best way. Amen.

# God Has a Family

**Let's Remember:**
"But as many as received Him, to them He gave the right to become children of God, even to those who believe in His name" (John 1:12).

**Let's Listen:**
You have two families! You belong to the family you live with. But you also belong to the family of God if you have asked Jesus to be your Savior. God's family is made up of all those who have invited Jesus into their lives. The Bible says that God gave those people the right to become His children. Everyone who has received Jesus as Lord and Savior is a child of God.

God knows that it's very hard to live without a family. That's why He has given us a big family called the church. When you gather with other Christians, they are more than friends. They are your brothers and sisters in Christ. We meet together each Sunday as a church to worship God.

Other Christians can help you live for Jesus, and you can help them do the same. That's why it's important to be with other Christians. When Christians get together to talk about how wonderful Jesus is, the Bible calls this *fellowship*.

### Let's Answer:

Question:   Why should you be with other Christians?

Answer:   Because Christians can help each other live for Jesus.

### Let's Talk About It:

Name some things we do at church that help us grow as Christians.

### Let's Pray Together:

Dear God, I'm glad to be part of Your wonderful family. Thank You for the chance to meet together with other Christians to worship You and to learn how we can serve You better. Amen.

# You Can Talk to God

**Let's Remember:**
" 'And whatever you ask in My name, that I will do, that the Father may be glorified in the Son' " (John 14:13).

**Let's Listen:**
Prayer is talking to God. We can talk to Him about anything. He loves for us to come to Him with all of our needs, joys, and dreams. He is always ready to listen.

We are to pray "in Jesus' name." This means we can ask for things from God as though Jesus Himself were asking. So we must always remember to ask for things that would please Jesus. When Jesus does what we ask, we see His power at work.

## Let's Answer:

Question:  What is prayer?
Answer:    Prayer is talking to God.

Question:  In whose name are you to pray?
Answer:    I am to pray in the name of Jesus.

## Let's Talk About It:

Look again at the wonderful promise Jesus made in John 14:13. What is something that will please God that hasn't happened yet? Ask God to make it happen in Jesus' name.

## Let's Pray Together:

Dear God, I'm asking You now to [place your request here]. I know that when You answer this request it will please You and Jesus, Your Son. So I ask You to answer my prayer because I am praying in Jesus' name. Amen.

# God Wrote You a Love Letter

**Let's Remember:**
"All Scripture is given by inspiration of God ..."
(2 Timothy 3:16).

**Let's Listen:**
God has written you a love letter! God's love letter to you is the Bible. In the Bible we find out how very much God loves us, even to the point of sending Jesus to die for us. The Bible tells us what God is like and how we can know Him.

There are no errors in the Bible. The Bible is God's Word and God cannot lie (read Titus 1:2 and Hebrews 6:18). The true church through history has always believed the Bible is correct. Though a few people have tried to prove that there are mistakes in the Bible, they have never been able to find even one!

Because God loves us He has given us a Book we can trust. It is His love letter to His children.

**Let's Answer:**
Question:   What does the Bible tell us?
Answer:     The Bible tells us what God is like and how we can know Him.

**Let's Talk About It:**
Have you ever received a card or a letter in the mail? Were you excited about hearing what it said? God has sent you a letter called the Bible, and He wants you to listen carefully to what He said.

**Let's Pray Together:**
Thank You, God, for Your Holy Word, the Bible. Teach me to respect, love, and obey it. In Jesus' name, amen.

# You Can Tell Others

**Let's Remember:**

"And He said to them, 'Follow Me, and I will make you fishers of men' " (Matthew 4:19).

**Let's Listen:**

If we know Jesus, we want to tell others about Him. The good news about Him is too wonderful not to share. When we tell others about Jesus, we feel a special joy inside. What could be more exciting than bringing someone else to Jesus so they can know Him too! Jesus says that if we follow Him, we will learn how to "fish for men," which is the same thing as telling others about Jesus.

The Bible says, "For I am not ashamed of the gospel of Christ, for it is the power of God to salvation for everyone who believes . . ." (Romans 1:16).

We should never be ashamed of the good news about Jesus. It's the best news the world will ever hear! How happy we are when we tell others about Jesus!

## Let's Answer:

Question:   If you follow Jesus what will you become?

Answer:   I will become a "fisher of men" (Matthew 4:19).

## Let's Talk About It:

Who are some people you know who need to hear the good news about Jesus? When will you tell them about Him?

## Let's Pray Together:

Thank You, Jesus, for letting me tell others about You. I'm glad that I can tell people the best news they will ever hear. Help me never to be afraid to talk to my friends about You. In Jesus' name, amen.

# VI.

## Jesus Taught Us How To Live

# Blessed Are
# the Poor in Spirit

*Let's Remember:*

" 'Blessed are the poor in spirit,/For theirs is the kingdom of heaven' " (Matthew 5:3).

*Let's Listen:*

One day Jesus taught a lot of people who gathered around Him on a mountainside. We call the message He gave the *Sermon on the Mount.* In that sermon Jesus told the people how to live so they would please God and be blessed.

When Jesus said we would be blessed if we followed His teachings, He meant we would be happy if we followed them. He said first, "Blessed [or happy] are the poor in spirit, for theirs is the kingdom of heaven." This means that those people who realize they are *not* good enough to come to God on their own are happy. Why? Because they are the only ones able to trust Jesus to bring them to God. And they will one day go to "the kingdom of heaven."

## Let's Answer:

Question: Is anyone good enough to get to heaven on his own?

Answer: No. We must trust in Jesus to bring us to God and to heaven.

## Let's Talk About It:

Some people think they're good enough to come to God without believing in Jesus. We call this "spiritual pride," which is sort of like bragging or thinking we're better than we really are. Jesus taught us to be "poor in spirit," to realize that we must have His goodness in us. Have you come to God as one who is "poor in spirit"?

## Let's Pray Together:

Dear God, I know I'm not good enough to come live with You in heaven. But I'm glad You will accept me anyway if I receive Jesus, Your Son. Help me to remember that I am "poor in spirit" so I can be happy and receive Your riches. In Jesus' name, amen.

# Blessed Are Those Who Mourn

**Let's Remember:**

" 'Blessed are those who mourn,/For they shall be comforted' " (Matthew 5:4).

**Let's Listen:**

Think of this! Jesus said that people who are sad can be blessed and happy. It is a good thing to be sad, if we are sad about the things that make God sad. A man once prayed, "Let my heart be broken by the things that break the heart of God."* Many of those who are sad now will one day rejoice.

Sad things happen in every person's life. When we are sad, we can feel that Jesus is very close to us. That's why Jesus said, "Blessed are those who mourn,/For they shall be comforted."

*The late Dr. Bob Pierce, founder of World Vision

*Let's Answer:*

Question:   When is a special time that we can feel Jesus is very close to us?

Answer:   We can feel Jesus is very close to us when we are sad.

*Let's Talk About It:*

Do you remember a very sad time in your life? Remember that Jesus wants to comfort you and be very close to you in times like that.

*Let's Pray Together:*

Thank You, Lord Jesus, that You don't leave Your children sad forever. You turn their sadness into joy. Sorrow is turned into joy before You.* Amen.

---

*Job 41:22

121

# Blessed Are the Gentle

**Let's Remember:**

" 'Blessed are the gentle,/For they shall inherit the earth' " (Matthew 5:5).

**Let's Listen:**

We've already learned that when we are gentle we will obey the Golden Rule. That Rule says, " 'Therefore, whatever you want [others] to do to you, you also do to them' " (Matthew 7:12).

Some people don't think it's smart to be gentle and to obey the Golden Rule. They think you should fight for everything and be mean if you need to be. That is how to get what you want, they say.

But we know better! Jesus promises that those who are gentle will inherit the earth some day. That's a present worth waiting for!

***Let's Answer:***

Question:   What will happen one day to those who are gentle?

Answer:   They will inherit the earth.

***Let's Talk About It:***

What does the Golden Rule say? What were some times when you obeyed this rule?

***Let's Pray Together:***

Thank You, Lord, for the wonderful future I have with You! Teach me to be gentle, so that I may inherit the earth. In Jesus' name, amen.

# Blessed Are Those Who Hunger and Thirst for Righteousness

**Let's Remember:**

" 'Blessed are those who hunger and thirst for righteousness,/For they shall be filled' " (Matthew 5:6).

**Let's Listen:**

When we're hungry, we want food. When we're thirsty, we want water. All people desire food and water from time to time. In a similar way, some people have a *great* desire to please God. That's what it means to hunger and thirst after righteousness. We can ask God to give us that desire. If you have that desire, it means you want to please God in all that you think, say, and do.

When we are filled with the Holy Spirit, we have God's power to live the kind of life we desire—a life pleasing to God.

**Let's Answer:**

Question:  What does it mean to hunger and thirst for righteousness?

Answer:  It means to desire to please God in all that I think, say, and do.

**Let's Talk About It:**

Do you want to please God in everything you think, say, and do? What are some ways you can please God?

**Let's Pray Together:**

Dear God, I want to please You with all of my heart. Fill me with Your Holy Spirit so I can have power to live a life that is pleasing to You. In Jesus' name, amen.

# Blessed Are the Merciful

**Let's Remember:**

" 'Blessed are the merciful,/For they shall obtain mercy' " (Matthew 5:7).

**Let's Listen:**

"He deserves to be punished!"

Have you ever heard anyone say that? Perhaps the person really did something wrong and deserves punishment. But how beautiful it is when we are kind and show mercy to such a person. To "show mercy" means to *not* punish someone who really deserves it and to forgive that person from the heart.

We should never forget that we deserve to be punished, too. We should be punished for our sins. But Jesus had mercy on us and took the punishment Himself! Just think how much He loves us.

Since Jesus showed mercy to us, we should show mercy to others. If we show mercy to others now, we will receive mercy later.

### Let's Answer:
Question: What is the reward for being merciful?
Answer: God will be merciful to us.

### Let's Talk About It:
Who can you show mercy to right now?

### Let's Pray Together:
Lord Jesus, You have been so merciful to me. You have forgiven all my sins and taken all my punishment. Help me now to be merciful to others. I ask this in Your name. Amen.

# Blessed Are the Pure in Heart

## Let's Remember:

" 'Blessed are the pure in heart,/For they shall see God' " (Matthew 5:8).

## Let's Listen:

When Jesus comes into our lives, He makes our heart—that secret part of ourselves that only God can see—clean and pure. If Jesus is in our life, we will one day see God the Father.

The prophet Jeremiah said, "The heart is deceitful above all things,/ And desperately wicked;/ Who can know it?" (Jeremiah 17:9). People's hearts are deceitful. That means that oftentimes we think it is better to do what is wrong instead of what God says. Evil ways and evil thoughts are natural when a person doesn't know Jesus. The person without Jesus may think and do things even he doesn't understand. Even those who love Jesus do and think wrong things, but they can and will change because Jesus lives in them.

After King David had sinned he prayed, "Create in me a clean heart, O God, and renew a steadfast spirit within me" (Psalm 51:10). God can give us a pure heart.

### Let's Answer:

Question: Who can make your heart clean and pure?

Answer: Jesus can make my heart clean and pure.

### Let's Talk About It:

Why does your heart need to be made clean and pure by Jesus? What does the Bible mean when it says our hearts are deceitful and wicked?

### Let's Pray Together:

Dear God, my prayer is the same as King David's prayer of long ago. "Create in me a clean heart, O God, and renew a steadfast spirit within me." In Jesus' name, amen.

# Blessed Are the Peacemakers

***Let's Remember:***

" 'Blessed are the peacemakers,/For they shall be called sons of God' " (Matthew 5:9).

***Let's Listen:***

A peacemaker is someone who tries to make enemies into friends. It is not always an easy job. Sometimes people who are angry at each other will become angry at a peacemaker too. This is what happened to Jesus, the Prince of Peace.

Our Bible verse promises that peacemakers will be called sons of God. Children of God are those who have Jesus living inside of them. Jesus brings peace and happiness into our lives. As children of God we want others to know this peace and happiness too. God has given us a special job of bringing peace between people who don't like each other. That's our job: turning enemies into friends!

### Let's Answer:

Question: What is the reward for the peace-maker?

Answer: The peacemaker will be called a son of God.

### Let's Talk About It:

Can you think of anyone you know who is angry with someone else? What can you do to help them be friends?

### Let's Pray Together:

Dear God, help people to know that I belong to You because I work at turning enemies into friends. In Jesus' name, amen.

# Blessed Are Those Who Are Persecuted for Righteousness' Sake

## Let's Remember:

" 'Blessed are those who are persecuted for righteousness' sake,/For theirs is the kingdom of heaven' " (Matthew 5:10).

## Let's Listen:

There are times when Christians are called upon to suffer for the name of Jesus. Peter, one of Jesus' disciples, said, "For to this you were called, because Christ also suffered for us, leaving us an example, that you should follow His steps" (1 Peter 2:21). It is a very high honor to suffer for Christ and the gospel. Some Christians lose their friends when they follow Jesus. Some Christians are laughed at. Others are cursed. Some are even killed because they stand up for Jesus.

You will be called upon to suffer for Jesus in some

way some day. Then you will know what it means to be "persecuted for righteousness' sake." You never need to be afraid of this. Those who suffer for Jesus know that He is with them. And just think of the reward! "For theirs is the kingdom of heaven."

### Let's Answer:
Question:  What is the reward for those who are persecuted for righteousness' sake?

Answer:  Theirs is the kingdom of heaven.

### Let's Talk About It:
Why should we never be afraid to suffer for Jesus? How can we be prepared to suffer for Jesus?

### Let's Pray Together:
Dear God, I know it is an honor to suffer for You and Your cause. Help me to never be afraid to live for You, whatever the cost. Help me to never be ashamed of You. I love You, Lord. Keep me true to You all the days of my life. In Jesus' name, amen.

# VII.

## Some Very Important Words

# Repentance

**Let's Remember:**
" '. . . Repent and believe the gospel' " (Mark 1:15).

**Let's Listen:**
Sin is anything in our lives that doesn't please God. It is not caring about what God wants and living just to please ourselves. When a person repents he stops living for himself and starts living for God. When a person repents he changes his mind about the way he should live.

Before we can really live as God desires, we must repent. That means we must stop living just to please ourselves. Then we will want to think and do only what will make God happy.

## Let's Answer:

Question: What happens when a person repents?

Answer: When a person repents he stops living just to please himself and starts living to please God.

## Let's Talk About It:

What are some thoughts or actions from which we should turn away?

## Let's Pray:

Dear God, I turn from anything in my life that doesn't please You. I turn to You and ask You to help me live in a way that pleases You. In Jesus' name, amen.

# Salvation

*Let's Remember:*
" 'For whoever calls upon the name of the Lord will be saved' " (Romans 10:13).

*Let's Listen:*
A person's most important need is for salvation. When a person asks God to forgive him for his sins and receives Jesus into his life, that person is saved.

First, he is saved from being punished for his sins. Punishment for sin means being put in a place far from God forever after death. But the Christian is saved from that penalty. "For God so loved the world that He gave His only begotten Son, that whoever believes in Him should not perish but have everlasting life" (John 3:16).

But the Christian is also saved so that he can live a

life pleasing to God. If Jesus lives inside of us, we live to please God.

## Let's Answer:

Question: What are Christians saved from?

Answer: Christians are saved from being punished for their sins.

Question: What are Christians able to do once they are saved?

Answer: Christians can learn to live a life pleasing to God.

## Let's Talk About It:

The word *salvation* means to be rescued out of some danger. What danger were we in before we invited Jesus into our lives?

## Let's Pray Together:

Thank You, Jesus, for taking the punishment for my sins by Your death on the cross. Thank You that I can be saved from the penalty of my sins by trusting You to save me. Help me to live a life that is pleasing to You. In Jesus' name, amen.

# Reverence

*Let's Remember:*

"God is greatly to be feared in the assembly of the saints,/And to be held in reverence by all those who are around Him" (Psalm 89:7).

*Let's Listen:*

To reverence God means to have a great respect for His power, His love, and His name. When the Bible tells us to fear God, it means we are to hold God in the very highest respect and honor as our heavenly Father. We should *never* take His name lightly nor joke about Him. He is *God*. He has the power to do anything. He can create storms and He can stop them. He can give life and He can take it. God created everything there is.

When we reverence God we are amazed at His

wonderful acts. We bow before Him in worship, love, and obedience.

**Let's Answer:**
Question: What does it mean to reverence God?
Answer: To reverence God means to have a great respect for His power, His love, and His name.

**Let's Talk About It:**
What are some ways you can show reverence for God?

**Let's Pray Together:**
Dear God, I bow in reverence before You. I praise You for Your power, Your love, and Your name. I love You and I respect You. In Jesus' name, amen.

# Obey

*Let's Remember:*

"Children, obey your parents in the Lord, for this is right" (Ephesians 6:1).

*Let's Listen:*

God has placed certain people in our lives whom we are to obey. He has done this because He loves us. These people are given to protect us and help us. Our parents, teachers, pastors, and policemen are all gifts to us from God. We are to obey what they tell us, unless what they tell us would make us sin against God. When we obey, we do what we are told to do. When we do this for the Lord, we show Jesus that we want to obey His Word, the Bible. Jesus said, " 'If you love Me, keep My commandments' " (John 14:15). We should always obey what God says in His Word.

There is a special promise for those who obey their parents. The Bible says they will have a long, happy life.

**Let's Answer:**

Question: What does the Bible promise, if you obey your parents?

Answer: I will have a long, happy life.

**Let's Talk About It:**

Name some people in your life you should obey. What is the one Book you should always obey?

**Let's Pray Together:**

Dear Lord, I pray that I will obey those You have placed over me to protect and help me. May I always obey Your Holy Word, the Bible. In Jesus' name, amen.

# Forgive

*Let's Remember:*

"Be kind to one another, tenderhearted, forgiving one another, just as God in Christ also has forgiven you" (Ephesians 4:32).

*Let's Listen:*

What do you do when someone is mean to you? Do you become angry and look for a way to be mean back? People who will not forgive others become hateful. Hateful people are never fun to be around. Hatefulness often makes people sick. Sometimes hatefulness makes people so sick they die. But most of all, when we do not forgive others we cannot become good friends with Jesus.

If you don't forgive when others treat you unfairly, you will become hateful. You won't have fun, and you won't be fun to be around. And we're never happy when we aren't close to Jesus. When we try to please Him, then we are truly happy.

Jesus has forgiven us for all our sins. Since He has forgiven us, we should forgive others.

### Let's Answer:
Question:   Why should you forgive others?

Answer:     I should forgive others because Jesus has forgiven me.

### Let's Talk About It:
Is there someone who has hurt you whom you need to forgive?

### Let's Pray Together:
Thank You, God, for forgiving me all my sins against You. Just as You have forgiven me for hurting You, I now forgive all those who have hurt me. Help me always to forgive quickly when I am wronged. In Jesus' name, amen.

# Love

**Let's Remember:**

" 'By this all will know that you are My disciples, if you have love for one another.' " (John 13:35).

**Let's Listen:**

People will know that we are Jesus' followers, His disciples, if we love one another. Everything about us should show love.

The apostle Paul told us what this love of God is like. "Love suffers long and is kind; love does not envy; love does not parade itself, is not puffed up; does not behave rudely, does not seek its own, is not provoked, thinks no evil; does not rejoice in iniquity, but rejoices in the truth; bears all things, believes all things, hopes all things, endures all things. Love never fails" (1 Corinthians 13:4–8).

When people see that kind of love in us they will know we are Jesus' disciples!

## Let's Answer:

Question: How will others know that you are Jesus' disciple?

Answer: If I show love for others.

## Let's Talk About It:

What are some ways you can show love to others? What first step should you take right now?

## Let's Pray Together:

Dear God, help me to love others as You do. Then everyone will know that I am a follower of Jesus. In His name, amen.

# Disciple

**Let's Remember:**

Jesus said ". . . 'If you continue in My word, then you are My disciples indeed' " (John 8:31).

**Let's Listen:**

A disciple is someone who is following Jesus. The word "disciple" means a "learner." A disciple is someone who is always learning more about Jesus and His ways.

Here are some things you can do to learn more about Jesus and His ways. You can talk to God in prayer. Tell Him everything you think about. You can listen to God's Word, the Bible. As you learn to read the Bible, the world's most wonderful book, you can tell others the good news about Jesus. Then they can know Him too. You can worship God with other

Christians at church. This is a time when we get to know others in God's big, wonderful family.

If you do these things, you will learn more about Jesus and His ways.

## Let's Answer:

Question:  What does it mean to be a disciple of Jesus?

Answer:  It means that I am following Jesus and learning more about Him and His ways.

## Let's Talk About It:

Let's name again the four ways we can learn more about Jesus and His ways.

## Let's Pray Together:

Dear God, help me to be a good follower of Jesus. Help me to always be learning more about Him and His ways. In Jesus' name, amen.

# Christian

*Let's Remember:*
". . . And the disciples were first called Christians in Antioch" (Acts 11:26).

*Let's Listen:*
A person is not a Christian just because he goes to church or is a church member. A person is not a Christian because he has been baptized or christened. A person is not a Christian because he does kind deeds. A Christian may do all of these things, but that is not what makes a person a Christian. *A Christian is a person who has Jesus Christ living inside of him.* If you can say honestly that Jesus is Lord of your life and if you believe that Jesus rose from the dead, you are a Christian and Jesus lives in you.

***Let's Answer:***

Question: What is a Christian?

Answer: A Christian is a person who has Jesus Christ living inside of him.

***Let's Talk About It:***

When people look at your life, can they tell that you are a Christian?

***Let's Pray Together:***

Lord Jesus, thank You for living inside of me. Teach me always how to live in such a way that people will know that I belong to You. In Your name, amen.

# Appendix

# What Christians
# Have Always Believed

***Let's Remember:***

I believe in God the Father Almighty, Maker of heaven and earth. And in Jesus Christ, His only Son our Lord; who was conceived by the Holy Ghost; born of the Virgin Mary; suffered under Pontius Pilate; was crucified, dead, and buried; He descended into hell; the third day He rose from the dead; He ascended into heaven; and sitteth on the right hand of God the Father Almighty; from thence He shall come to judge the quick and the dead. I believe in the Holy Ghost, the holy catholic church, the communion of saints, the forgiveness of sins; the resurrection of the body; and the life everlasting. Amen.*

---

*Parents should help children understand words whose meanings may be difficult or archaic. For instance, "catholic" means "universal" and is not a reference to any particular denomination.

## Let's Listen:

A creed is a statement of what people believe. Long ago some Christians decided they should write down some of their most important beliefs. This was done to help them stay away from false teachings that did not say the same things the Bible says.

What we have read is known as the Apostles' Creed. For many hundreds of years Christians have been reciting this creed to remind them of some of their most important beliefs.

Today as Christians we are linked in faith with all those who have believed in Jesus for almost two thousand years. It's an honor to be part of that large group of people through the centuries who belong to Jesus. Let's recite the Apostles' Creed again.

## Let's Answer:

Question: What is the Apostles' Creed?

Answer: The Apostles' Creed is a statement of some of the most important beliefs of the Christian church.

## Let's Talk About It:

What are some words in this creed that you don't understand? Let's talk about what they mean.

### Let's Pray Together:

Thank You, Father, that the truth about You and the truth about Jesus never changes. I'm glad my faith rests in beliefs that have always been true and always will be. Amen.

# Some Favorite Bible Stories

───────────

*Acts 6–7 gives the full story of Stephen for older children.

After reading this book,
please give it
to someone you love.